Praise for *I Love You More Than Coffee*

"Warm, wise, and easy to read, this collection of essays is a primer for parenthood that will charm your soul. *I Love You More Than Coffee* does a masterful job of tip-toeing through everyday life with babies, kids, new homes, in-laws, careers, and so much more. Melissa Face's style is delightful and unobtrusive—her writing never gets in the way of the lovely story she's telling."
Karen Schwartzkopf, editor, *Richmond Family Magazine*

"In *I Love You More Than Coffee*, author Melissa Face explores the joys and hardships of motherhood, from the horrific realization the smell of her beloved drink gives her morning sickness to the meaningful moments she might never have experienced without her children's influence. Just like a cup of flavored coffee, it leaves you with a warm feeling in your soul."
Charity Bishop, editor, *Prairie Times*

"I couldn't put down *I Love You More Than Coffee*. Melissa Face's thought-provoking collection blends humor with heart to tell the compelling narrative of motherhood, a narrative that is both personal and universal and will stick with you long after reading it."
Lindsay A. Chudzik, editor-in-chief, *Feels Blind Literary*

"As a soon-to-be first-time mom, it's nice to read a book about having kids that is really relatable. Melissa Face's essay collection is exactly what I need at this stage in my life and something that anyone who is a parent will absolutely love."
Kris Perelmutter, author and television personality

"On days when you feel like the superwoman myth might literally kill you, or when you think you might have to auction your child on eBay, pick up Melissa Face's *I Love You More Than Coffee*. These finely-crafted vignettes about the fears and joys of motherhood could bring on laughter or tears, but they will most assuredly inspire you to accept the help and wisdom of others, bloom where you are planted, and draw like the Mommy van Gogh your kids swear that you are."
Cindy L. Cunningham, PhD, author, *Bittersweet Swallows*

"Melissa Face's *I Love You More Than Coffee* percolated my very own precious mommy memories. Face's collection of true experiences she brewed to pour into our minds are filled with wit and life lessons. The final paragraphs in Face's chapters are worthy of becoming inspirational wall art in coffee bars across the globe."
Kristi K. Higgins, The Social Butterfly Columnist, *The Progress-Index*

"An honest, heartwarming, and hilarious look at motherhood. If you're about to be a mother, in the trenches, or looking back, this is the perfect book for you."
Elizabeth Varel, editor, *Parhelion Literary Magazine*

"When you read her essays, you are invited in to meet the real Melissa—and she is irresistible. This book, a collection of her very best writing on motherhood, is a must-read for all of us who love children. At times, being a mom is a very lonely and frustrating job, but it is also one of the most important roles we, as women, play. Melissa normalizes the bad days and shares her joy in the best parts of motherhood. I cried, I laughed, and I related completely to every single story. Bravo Melissa, for sharing your journey so honestly."
Leslie Moore, editor, Strand Media Group

"Melissa Face writes with honesty and humor about the joys and challenges of parenting. Her essays celebrate the daily struggles of being a young working mother along with surprising moments of insight and awareness that also come from parenthood. This collection is perfect for someone who is worried about what it might mean to have children, who might be worried about giving up their identity—and their sanity. For fans of Erma Bombeck or Nora Ephron, Melissa Face's *I Love You More Than Coffee* will reassure you that while it might be messy and exhausting and challenging, parenthood is also hilarious and sweet and well worth the trouble."
Patricia Smith, author, *The Year of Needy Girls*

I LOVE YOU MORE
THAN COFFEE

www.mascotbooks.com

I Love You More Than Coffee

Back cover photos taken by Scott Schwartzkopf

Author photo taken by Steve Werner, Pipe Dream Photography

For more information, please contact:
Mascot Books
620 Herndon Parkway #320
Herndon, VA 20170
info@mascotbooks.com

Library of Congress Control Number: 2019909906

CPSIA Code: PRFRE1019A
ISBN-13: 978-1-64543-086-5

Printed in Canada

for
EVAN
and
DELANEY

In memory of Mammie, who always loved a strong cup of coffee.

I LOVE YOU MORE THAN COFFEE

Essays on Parenthood

MELISSA FACE

TABLE OF CONTENTS

INTRODUCTION

THIS COLLECTION SPANS my first eight years of motherhood, beginning in early 2010, when I stood in my bathroom and celebrated a positive pregnancy test. Each essay was written in real time, or very close to it, so what you read is an authentic viewpoint from that particular phase in my life. Many of those years were difficult and isolating, and I coped by writing, attempting to sort out and make sense of my experiences.

I also credit my survival of the early years to coffee. Pots and pots of coffee.

In fact, coffee was such a big part of my introduction to motherhood that both of my children recognized the Starbucks logo long before they identified colors and basic shapes. My older child, Evan, believed for a long time that I went to work "to drink coffee." He was partly right.

I Love You More Than Coffee is perfect for parents who love coffee a lot and their kids...just a little more. It is a collection that moms and dads all over the world will relate to, with themes of exhaustion, worry, guilt, and giving ourselves a break from the daily tasks of parenting and from the guilt trips and negative self-talk. The collection highlights the challenges of raising a family while maintaining an identity, as well as the unconditional love we have for our children.

I had been looking for a way to package my essay collection when my daughter approached me with an interesting question: "Do you like me more than candy?" she asked. Naturally, I told her I did. She followed that question with, "Do you like me more than coffee?" I paused, feigned uncertainty, then laughed and squeezed her. I knew I had my title essay, as well as the title of my collection.

My essays, much like my taste in coffee, have evolved over the years. They started off light and sweet and became bolder and more flavorful as I have adapted to motherhood. Whether you read individual essays as little sips or gulp down the entire collection at once, I hope you enjoy it.

AT FIRST THERE IS WORRY

"CRAIG!" I YELLED. "Come downstairs!"

My husband, still half asleep, followed my voice into the bathroom. I was standing by the sink, holding a white stick in my hand.

"Look," I said. "Do you see two lines?"

"Yes," my husband answered.

"Really? You definitely see TWO lines?"

"Two lines. For sure," Craig confirmed. He smiled, kissed my forehead, and returned to bed.

I hopped in the shower and prepared for my day. I felt giddy. I wanted to run outside and tell everyone in my neighborhood, "I'm pregnant! I'm finally going to have a baby!"

That's what I wanted to do, but the calmer, smaller, more rational version of myself decided to wait out the next three months without making any major announcements. I knew it would be difficult to keep quiet, but it was the right thing to do.

Other than the positive test, my first sign of pregnancy was fatigue. I felt tired immediately after waking up, and the drowsiness continued throughout the day. It was not unusual for me to nod off at my desk or yawn in the middle of an important conversation.

Then came the nausea. It was subtle at first and easily soothed by a glass of ginger ale. But by six weeks, the queasiness was overwhelming. Once a two-cup per day coffee drinker, I suddenly couldn't tolerate the smell of it brewing. I also couldn't be in the presence of green vegetables, and I found any dish containing tomatoes completely repulsive.

I felt terrible and wonderful at the same time. I had pains in strange places, flu-like symptoms and headaches. But I also felt more alive than ever before, more in tune with my body, and more connected with nature.

There was another emotion that I experienced from the very beginning—worry. From the moment I saw the positive pregnancy test, I felt terrified that something might go wrong. I was familiar with the statistics on miscarriage in the first trimester, and I anxiously awaited that thirteen-week mark.

At my nine-week appointment, I had the typical series of tests and blood work. After being poked and prodded for about an hour, the doctor asked me if I would like to see what my "little one" was up to.

"Really? My first ultrasound?" I asked.

"Well, it would probably be nice if you experienced something pleasant at your first appointment," he chuckled.

My doctor placed the wand on my belly and pointed to the monitor. And there, in the middle of the screen, was a tiny, wriggling baby.

I asked my doctor if the baby looked okay and he said, "So far, so good."

What I wanted him to say was, "Everything is fine and you are going to deliver a perfectly healthy baby in approximately seven months."

That's what I wanted to hear, but it wasn't what I was told. I know that no doctor can guarantee a seamless pregnancy, an uncomplicated delivery, or a healthy child. I also realize that excessive worry will not tip the odds in my favor.

I am now twenty weeks along: I have reached the halfway point of my pregnancy. In the next few days, I will find out my baby's gender. Additionally, I will have some tests that detect certain abnormalities. I could obsess and worry about these screenings, but I am trying not to.

Throughout the years, there will always be something to worry about. I will be just as concerned when my child is behind the wheel of his first car as I am while he develops in my womb. I will worry when he naps in his crib and when he sleeps at a friend's house. There will be plenty to agonize over in the future, so I am going to take the next few months off.

At this moment, I am choosing to be happy and grateful for this pregnancy, for the fact that there is new life blooming inside of me. It is wonderful and beautiful.

I am having a baby.

WAITING ON A BABY

Tiny pajamas and outfits have been washed, folded, and organized by size. Various colored onesies are in drawers next to itty-bitty socks, shoes, and hats. Stacks of diapers line the shelves of the changing table next to rows of ointment, powder, and lotion. They wait to be used on a brand-new bottom that will arrive any day now.

My husband has spent evenings assembling the furniture, car seat, and stroller. He flipped through pages of Japanese directions, fought with numerous tools, and swore at that last bolt that remained on the floor, homeless. Then he proudly placed each item in the baby's nursery, where it will wait until it is needed.

The nursery is painted a lively green, and I stand here and stare at all of the wonderful gifts from people who love my husband, our baby, and me. I walk over to my glider chair, a gift from my in-laws, and place my unrecognizably swollen feet on the ottoman. I rest and rock for a while, knowing that this will be the last time I sit in this chair alone.

I gaze at his stuffed animals and flip through the pages of books that I cannot wait to read to him: *Goodnight Moon*, *The Poky Little Puppy*, and *Fox in Socks*. I listen to his personalized CD from Grandma and smile as I picture him, when he is older, clapping his hands and dancing to "Wake Up, Evan!" and "Do You Want to Go to the Zoo, Evan?"

I dust the top of his dresser that holds his piggy bank and rattle. They all surround a lovely blue picture frame that has the inscription, "Bless This Child." The frame sits empty, waiting to hold a photograph of my baby's beautiful face.

After a few more moments in the nursery, I return downstairs to check and recheck my hospital bags. They have been packed for weeks, but I constantly add more as the big day approaches. I include my copy of *What to Expect*, with its worn cover and dog-eared pages. I pack several issues of *Pregnancy* magazine, so I can soak up a few more pieces of advice while I pass the time in the hospital.

For the past several months, I have listened to tales of labor and delivery from family members, friends, and co-workers. They have told me of easy deliveries, thirty-six-hour labors, and emergency Caesareans. I have heard about back labor, epidurals that wore off, and painful episiotomies. I have been told what to expect, what to ask for, and how I will feel.

But these are their stories. I will soon have my own.

Yesterday, I said goodbye to my students and co-workers. My fifth block class threw me a goodbye party because they wanted me to "go out in style." They covered the whiteboard with well wishes and "we'll miss you" notes. They brought in homemade brownies, cookies, and cupcakes.

I turned over my laptop and lesson plans to my long-term substitute. I emptied my inbox, cleaned off my desk, and hugged my friend Sarah. I pulled out of the parking lot feeling completely confident in only one thought: my life will not be the same when I return to work in ten weeks.

I am prepared to go without sleep, worry constantly, feel incompetent, and love like I never have before. I am also prepared to rely on the help and support of my mother and others in my life who have the experience I lack.

Now I am home and officially on maternity leave. I have cleaned and organized everything possible. There is little left to do but wait. And that is exactly what I am doing. Like so many expectant mothers before me, I am sitting and waiting on the arrival of my newborn. Any day now, my life will be changed forever and for the better, because of my child.

EVERYTHING IN ITS PLACE

IT IS THREE O'CLOCK in the morning, and I am watching an infomercial for some sort of robotic vacuum cleaner. I am tempted to order it, in hopes that it will suck up the cookie crumbs in the kitchen and the mound of partially-chewed dog food in the hallway. Perhaps it could restore my home to a state somewhere near normalcy. But the phone is on the other side of the living room, my credit card is in my purse, and I am just too tired to move.

For the past three weeks, I have had no more than five consecutive hours of sleep. I nap for thirty minutes or so when I can, and I enjoy a longer, three-hour rest when my husband returns from work. I am exhausted, in need of a shower, and surrounded by complete chaos. I am a new mom, and this is my new life.

I expected to go days without sleep. I was prepared to deplete my checking account for weekly purchases of diapers and wipes. I was prepared to feel a bit overwhelmed with the newness of motherhood. I even expected the hours of nonstop crying—I just thought it would all come from the baby. But I was not prepared for my world to become completely disorganized.

My husband and I preferred living in an environment in which everything was in its place. Our house was far from perfect, but we did like our things clean and out of sight. This was important to our former selves.

Now, a glance around our house reveals a markedly different lifestyle. The coffee table is littered with empty bottles and burp cloths. The kitchen counter is covered with plates of half-eaten food and mugs of cold coffee. The diaper pail and laundry basket are overflowing, and the answering machine blinks with unheard messages.

Today, I woke up at six o'clock so I would have time to take a shower before my husband left for work. I quickly dressed, dried my hair, and ate some cereal. The baby began fussing, so I changed his diaper. The diaper change soon turned into a full bath and a new outfit.

I realized the baby was out of clean sleepers, so I wrapped him in a blanket and started a load of laundry. Then it was time to feed him, burp him, and lay him down for a nap. While he was sleeping, I tried to pay a few bills. I wrote one check, then the crying began again.

The baby's diaper was wet and so was his blanket. I went to grab a clean outfit and remembered I never dried the clothes. I wrapped the baby in another blanket and moved the wet laundry into the dryer.

Over the next few hours, we went through five more diaper changes and two additional outfits. The baby spent the remainder of the day eating and crying.

I did, too.

Before I knew it, my husband was coming in the back door after a long day at work. He walked into the kitchen and set down his keys and travel mug.

"How was your day?" he asked. "What have you been up to?"

I looked around at the pile of dishes, stack of bills, wet laundry, and other unfinished tasks around the house.

"I have taken care of the baby," I said. "I fed the baby,

burped the baby, held the baby, changed the baby, and bathed the baby. That is what I did today."

My husband sat down on the couch and put his arm around me.

"Go take a nap," he said. "I'll take over for a while."

I looked at him, our dog, and our beautiful baby boy. I realized that my house is still in order. Paperwork hasn't been filed, and laundry isn't folded. But everything is in its place, and I can quickly find all that I need. And right now, all three of them are on the couch.

SLEEPLESS NIGHTS

MOM WASTED NO TIME returning my phone call.

"Don't put the baby on eBay," she urged. "I'll be over in an hour to give you a break."

She hurried to my house, removed my screaming newborn from my arms, and proceeded to rock and sing to her grandchild while I took a nap.

It was a well-deserved rest. I had gone without a good night's sleep for the first four weeks of my child's life. While everyone else in the world counted sheep, I counted down the minutes until the baby's next feeding. That was when the room would finally be peaceful again. Then, in the early morning hours, I burped, changed, and rocked my baby as the sun rose on a new day.

There were times when my fatigue caused me to be a bit short-tempered with my mom—a very silly thing to do when someone is offering help.

"You are not the only new mother who has ever felt stressed and overwhelmed," she reminded me. "We've all been there."

My mom told me about spending late nights and early mornings in the rocking chair. "There were times when I tried everything to get you to stop fussing. I was at the end of my rope. But those days passed quickly for me. They will for you, too."

I knew she was right. It would pass quickly—too quickly—

then there would be other reasons for staying up all hours of the night: driver's licenses, proms, dates, etc.

I remember coming home a little late from a date when I was about sixteen. I slid my key in the lock, quietly turned the door knob, and closed the door behind me. I dodged the squeaky floorboards in the dining room and headed toward my room. Then, a light flicked on, and there sat my mother, waiting for me in the living room.

"Where have you been?" she demanded. "You were supposed to be home at eleven o'clock."

"It's only midnight," I argued. "What difference does an hour make?"

My mom grounded me for arguing with her and for breaking my curfew. She tried to make me understand that she was only angry with me because she was worried. I thought she was hateful and unfair, and it would take me years to realize otherwise.

There were several other occasions when my mom went without sleep because of me. She tossed and turned when I moved out of state, and she undoubtedly paced the halls when I announced that I had withdrawn from college. I kept her awake with the kind of worry that only a mother can feel.

It's four o'clock on a Wednesday morning, and my baby and I are wide-awake. He has eaten and has been changed, but he will not stop fussing unless I hold him. So, together, we sway in the rocking chair, his tiny head against my chest and my head drooping from exhaustion.

Years from now, I will be awake for other reasons. He will be late for curfew, driving for the first time, or going away to college. I will wonder where he is and whether or not he is okay. I will long for the late nights and early mornings that we spent together in the rocking chair.

Then, when the sun rises and the rest of the world is awake again, I will call my mother. She will understand.

MY TIME

I DIDN'T REALIZE how selfish I was until my son was born last year. As it turns out, I really enjoy the luxury of a hot shower each day. I also like being able to drink an entire cup of coffee while it's still hot. And every now and then, it's nice to get more than three consecutive hours of sleep. Who knew I was so self-centered?

There's nothing like having a child to remind you that you are no longer the center of your own universe. I understand that now. Evan's needs take precedence over mine on a daily basis. He eats first, he gets the first bath, and he decides when everyone else in the house will start the day.

Most days, being second doesn't bother me a bit. But every now and then, I have to recharge; I need the occasional "me" time.

That was how I felt back in June, when my mom and I booked an overnight trip to Dover, Delaware. We left on a Thursday afternoon, had a quick dinner on the road, and arrived in Delaware right after sunset. Mom and I settled into our hotel room and went downstairs to explore the casino. I found a slot machine that looked fun, then I ordered myself a drink. I had taken two sips (honestly) when I noticed my cell phone vibrating inside my purse. The call was from my husband.

"I'm so sorry to bother you," Craig said softly. "The baby is burning up and we are on the way to the hospital. He won't drink his bottle, and his temperature is 102."

I didn't know how to reply. I'd been so desperate to get away, take a break, and indulge a little. And now my baby was sick, and I couldn't do a thing for him. The situation made me feel helpless.

"I don't know what to do," I told him. "I'm five hours from home."

"I know," Craig said. "You can't help that. I'll call you when I know what's wrong."

Craig and my father took the baby to the emergency room. Meanwhile, I searched the casino for my mom. Once I found her, we went to our hotel room and waited...

Over an hour later, Craig called to tell me that the baby had bronchitis. He was on an antibiotic and already seemed to be feeling better. He was going to be just fine.

After vowing to never go anywhere without my baby again, I slept for a couple hours so we would be prepared for the drive home the next morning.

By the time I returned home, the baby was already back to his typical, happy self. He was playing in his bouncy seat and gnawing on a teething ring. Still, I didn't leave his side for several days.

Ever since this incident, I have struggled with the concept of "me" time. I've tried to figure out why I needed a break from the child I'd wanted so badly and love so very much. Why did I need to get away from a baby who smiles when he sees me, laughs when I sing like Elmo, and turns his head toward my voice, regardless of how many people are in the room?

Maybe it was because the same beautiful child demands my undivided attention, requires constant supervision, and sometimes renders me completely exhausted. Sometimes I need to feel like a person and not a bottle-making, diaper-changing, bath-giving, mommy machine.

In recent months, I have taken "me" time in small doses. My mom has kept the baby so I could grocery shop, take a nap, and clean my house. On a couple of occasions, Craig and I went to dinner with friends. And over the summer, I even managed to read an entire novel while the baby rested. It felt great to immerse myself in a different world for a while.

I'm still not ready to leave the baby overnight again or travel a long distance without him. It's too soon, and it makes me too anxious. But I do give myself a break when I need it; breaks are healthy for both of us.

I remember when I first announced my pregnancy, a friend told me to do whatever I wanted while I could. "There is no 'me' in mommy," she said.

There is a "my," though. So, I will take my time.

MUSH BRAIN

RETURNING TO THE CLASSROOM after ten weeks of maternity leave was one of the biggest challenges I have ever faced. It wasn't just the pain of being physically separated from my child, though that was quite intense. It was being caught completely off-guard by my new, and not-at-all improved, mush brain.

I thought motherhood was going to be a breeze. I'd worked three jobs while attending college; I'd worked the night shift at a television station while taking graduate classes; I'd managed to return to school to earn a teaching certification while I was pregnant. I was not a novice multitasker. So, how much additional work could a little baby be? I could handle it.

My first few weeks of motherhood had been a rude awakening. My son was sweet, handsome, and wonderful. He was everything I'd hoped he would be—with one exception. He had his own little schedule, and he didn't give a rip about mine.

So, after weeks of sleepless nights on maternity leave (I'd previously referred to it as baby vacation! Ha!), I prepared for my return to the classroom. I picked out a few non-maternity outfits, looked over my lesson plans, and packed my work bag.

My first day back was pretty painless. I returned on a teacher workday. Aside from a few meetings and in-service trainings, I spent the day catching up with co-workers. My co-teachers updated me on student progress, minor changes in the curriculum, and which students were currently on the suspension list. I was ready for my first day back in the classroom.

But the next morning, when kids began filing in, I felt like I was seeing them for the first time. I couldn't remember anyone's name. Students approached me and told me they were glad to have me back. I smiled and thanked them, reluctant to call them by name because I was sure I would get it wrong.

At my next check-up, I talked to my doctor about memory loss. He explained that it was a pretty common post-pregnancy occurrence. I asked him how long it would last, and he told me that the jury was still out on that one.

My failing memory wasn't isolated to student names. I had forgotten vocabulary words, literary terms, names of co-workers, and my own schedule. I decided to make cheat sheets for everything until my memory and processing skills began to improve.

While my memory aids were helpful, they didn't prevent me from walking into my classroom with formula stains on my pants, or carrying my child's diaper bag into the building instead of my teaching bag.

But it wasn't helpful to beat myself up for everything I was doing wrong; I needed to cut myself a break. Instead of worrying about what was on my pants, I needed to be grateful that I'd left the house wearing a pair. After all, I was a new mom, and even the simplest tasks were overwhelming.

Eventually, my mush brain improved, and I felt like a competent teacher again. I established a routine, and with the help of my husband, co-workers, and parents, I made it through the rest of the year successfully.

Today, multitasking doesn't have exactly the same meaning for me that it used to. Some days I accomplish a lot, and some days I simply get by. When I am able to schedule a doctor's appointment during my lunch break and grade a few papers while my child naps, I consider that a major accomplishment. And then there are days when I take a nap with him, and that's okay, too.

In fact, it's more than okay. It's necessary, for my memory and for me. It's preventive medicine, fighting off a relapse of mommy mush brain.

MOMMY VAN GOGH

"DRAW," SAYS EVAN, my nineteen-month-old.

His tiny hand grasps the red crayon and moves it back and forth across the lined paper. I clap for him, tell him he is doing a great job, and his round face lights up. He is proud.

"Draw. Draw. Draw," he repeats.

Evan continues marking the paper with the red crayon, and I keep reinforcing how wonderful his artwork is. And it is wonderful. Evan is my firstborn, so, by nature, everything he does is just wonderful.

Then, Evan does the unthinkable. He takes the red crayon and the notebook and shoves them both in my direction. He looks at me with hopeful eyes and says, "Draw, Mama."

Oh no, I think to myself. *I was afraid of this.*

I have dreaded this moment for a long time. I am terrible at artwork. I have always been terrible at artwork.

In elementary school, my classmates skipped down the breezeway when it was time for art class. I hung back at the end of the line and walked slowly. Less time in class meant fewer opportunities to embarrass myself with another horrific creation.

Throughout the years, I painted, sculpted, and drew as required. And since it was elementary school, I was given passing grades on my creations. I brought home numerous stick-figure drawings, paint smears, misshapen globs of clay, and papier-mâché distortions. And like all good parents would, my mom and dad praised my artwork and displayed it somewhere in the house.

I remember making a butterfly in Bible school, a candle at youth camp, and a cloth heart at Mission Friends. My parents lovingly placed each item on the desk in their study. I shuddered when I walked past their little desktop gallery. I knew I wasn't an artist.

I am thirty-three years old now, and little has changed in terms of my artistic abilities. I have not progressed past stick-figure drawing; I can't cut out a heart shape from a folded piece of paper; I am incapable of neatly folding the corners of a gift-wrapped package.

But today, my toddler wants me to draw. He insists that I draw. So, to avoid letting him down, I pick up the red crayon and begin. I draw a smiley face. Evan laughs. Then, I draw a sun in the corner of the paper. Evan keeps smiling.

"Draw, Mama," he repeats.

I get braver and attempt one of my trademark stick-figure people.

"Da-Da!" he squeals.

With a little more confidence, I draw another stick-figure next to the first one. It has a triangle dress and long lines of hair.

"Ma-Ma!" Evan squeals again and claps his hands.

Clearly, my drawings are better than I thought.

This is not as unpleasant as I feared. In fact, I am starting to have a little bit of fun. I draw a picture of our dog, Tyson, beside the two figures.

"Horsey!" Evan shouts.

Close enough.

For the next few minutes, Evan and I engage in our own version of Pictionary. I attempt to draw something that he recognizes, and he shouts out the object's name. Sometimes I am successful, and sometimes I fall short. But regardless of the quality of the finished product, each of my attempts is met with an appreciative giggle or squeal.

Today, I am an artist.

Now I know that I do possess a little artistic talent. I had just never met with my ideal audience until the other day. I am meant to draw only for the non-judgmental, inexperienced, completely open-minded toddler. My work is meant to be displayed on Etch A Sketches, Magna Doodles, and coloring books throughout my home. I am particularly creative with stickers, magic markers, and of course, red crayons.

I am an artist. I am Mommy van Gogh.

TIME TO PLAY

I HAVE BEEN inundated with parental advice from the moment I first announced my pregnancy. Friends and co-workers offered me tips about diet, daycare, and health insurance long before my precious bundle even entered the world. The most popular piece of advice came at me from nearly every direction: "Sleep while you can," people repeated, as though women in their third trimesters of pregnancy really sleep soundly.

But months later, I knew exactly what they meant.

When I returned to work from maternity leave, co-workers kindly asked me how I was adjusting to motherhood.

"I feel like I can't get anything done like I used to," I told them. "My house is a disaster, the bills are piling up, and I haven't had a moment to myself since Evan was born."

"Welcome to motherhood!" they laughed. "You will never get things done like you used to. That's just the way it is."

Feeling less than comforted by the conversation, I headed back to my work area. I felt someone grab my arm and I turned around. A teacher named Vicki told me to follow her.

"Look," she began. "I know you're probably getting plenty of advice, but I want to tell you one thing that I wish someone had told me."

"Go ahead," I encouraged. "I'm definitely open to suggestions."

"Let the dishes pile up," she said. "Let the laundry accumulate. Do less housework than you ever have before, even though there is more to do than ever before."

"What?" I asked, flabbergasted. I was expecting a magic formula for increased efficiency and productivity.

"I'm serious," she continued. "Let go of the housework and spend time with your baby. I spent too much time worrying about laundry and dishes. Those things just don't matter."

As summer break approached, I became more excited about spending ten weeks with my toddler. I was looking forward to day trips, lunches, afternoon naps, and mornings at the neighborhood pool. I wanted to sit on the floor and play with trucks, tractors, and trains. I wanted to watch *Clifford*, *The Cat in the Hat*, and *Curious George*. I knew it was going to be a great summer.

I thought about Vicki's advice from earlier in the spring and decided to shrug off my domestic duties, at least temporarily. When I put Evan down for his nap in the Pack 'n Play one afternoon, I thought about the dishes, the laundry, and the dirty floors. I could easily get those things taken care of while Evan napped. But I decided not to. Instead, I climbed in my bed next to his Pack 'n Play. Today, we were both going to take a nap.

"Hi, Mama!" Evan squealed. He turned to watch me lie down and adjust my pillow. "Play?" he asked, hopefully.

"No, buddy," I told him. "It's nap time. Go night night."

For a few minutes, he flipped and squirmed, attempting to make himself comfortable. After a while, he seemed to forget I was in the room. Then, he twirled his blanket around his head and his voice became softer and softer as he repeated, "Tractor, truck, big truck, yay! Tractor, truck, big truck, yay!"

I was grateful to be in the room at that moment, witnessing his sleepy baby monologue. And at the same time, I had to hide my face in the pillow to keep from laughing.

Eventually, Evan fell asleep and I did, too. We both woke up a couple of hours later, happy and hungry. We had snacks and played and watched tractor videos until my husband came home from work.

That night, once we put the baby to bed, I picked up the toys and books that littered the floor. My husband and I cleaned up the kitchen and discussed our days. I told him about naptime with Evan. And while a small part of me wished I had taken better care of the house that day, a much larger part realized I had done exactly what I was supposed to do.

I was fortunate to receive a really great piece of advice as a new mom, and I have thought about it every day since. Right now, there is a blanket of dust covering my entertainment center and there are tiny fingerprints on my sliding glass window. I need to clean the house, but it will have to wait. Evan is pulling the truck out of his toy basket, and we need to play.

BLOOM WHERE YOU'RE PLANTED

AFTER A PEACEFUL eight hours of sleep, I wake up, run a mile or two on my treadmill, take a shower, and dress. Then, I prepare breakfast for Evan. Sometimes we have pancakes or waffles, and some days we eat cereal. Today, he chooses Cheerios.

I enjoy a couple of cups of coffee while he eats, and we plan our day. I dress Evan in his favorite train shirt, jeans, and light-up fire truck shoes, and we watch an episode of *Super Why*. Then, we dance to the Wiggles, crawl on the floor like dogs, and roar like dinosaurs. We do everything Evan wants, and it is an ideal morning.

Before we know it, it's lunch time. Evan requests macaroni and cheese, green beans, and applesauce. Since that is right in line with my culinary skills, he gets his wish. We eat, make funny faces, and laugh. Life is good.

After lunch, Evan takes a two-hour nap, and I spend that time reading, writing a new essay, and organizing a couple of closets. I am amazed at how productive I can be while he rests.

Evan wakes up and we go outside. He wants to drive his Little Tikes fire truck, blow bubbles, and talk to our neighbors. I am so happy to have time to chat, breathe the fresh air, and watch my child play. Life couldn't be better.

Or could it?

While I have lived this particular day, it is not my typical routine.

In reality, I get about five or six hours of sleep, wake up, shower, pour my coffee into a travel mug, and head out the door. Some days, I am at work before my husband and child have gotten out of bed. Other days, I get to give them each a quick kiss before heading to my car.

Each day, I teach high school English for about seven hours, attend meetings, drive to pick up my child, and start the evening routine of dinner, play time, bathtime, bedtime, lesson planning, grading, and preparing for the next day. It is an exhausting whirlwind of a schedule that often leaves me wishing for a different life, a life much like the one I first described.

This is what happens when I spend too much time staring at the lush, green grass on the other side of the fence. It appears perfect and maintenance-free. But it's not. Every lifestyle requires a certain degree of work, and every child-rearing scenario has the potential for stress. I know this, but I often need a reminder.

I have spent hours calculating my family's expenses, trying to find a way to survive on one income. I still can't make it work for us. I have stayed up late reading articles about the pros and cons of staying at home and working outside the home. The only thing I really learned from my research is that there is an abundance of literature that both supports and criticizes any decision a person could choose to make.

While I ponder my decisions and current situation, a certain phrase keeps popping into my head: bloom where you're planted. My grandmother gave me this advice a long time ago, and she said her mother used to say it to her. It really is great advice, and it summarizes everything I need to do in terms of making the most of my situation.

While I am at work, my child is with a caring sitter whose

home is just down the street from ours, and two days per week, he is with my parents. Evan is verbal, social, and very well adjusted. He loves his daycare buddies, and he enjoys the individual attention from my parents.

And he is loved—immensely.

Since I teach, I have weekends, holiday breaks, and summers at home with Evan. I do get a taste of the stay-at-home mom life from time to time, and I love it.

My vivacious toddler is happy wherever he is. He looks for the good things in every environment, and I need to do the same. I need to spend less time worrying and more time savoring moments with Evan.

Childhood, and life in general, pass far too quickly. I can't waste any more time watching the grass in other people's yards. I'm going to dig deep into the soil of my life—and bloom.

BABY EVAN

IN MY EFFORT to hang on to each moment of his childhood for as long as possible, I have continued to call my son "Baby Evan," even though he no longer qualifies as a baby. And now that he has become a walking, talking, two-year-old, he understandably refers to himself by the same name.

"Well, hello there, young man," says a kind lady in the grocery store. "What is your name?"

"I'm Baby Evan," he proudly responds.

The lady laughs, pats him on the head, and continues down the aisle.

"Aren't you just the cutest!" remarks the cashier at Target. "What is your name?"

"I'm Baby Evan," he says, without hesitation.

And so it goes. Each time he is asked, his response is the same. It has been very cute for quite some time, but my husband and I are beginning to worry. We discuss ways of getting him to drop the "baby," and we talk about the possible consequences of him not giving up this title. He might scoot through elementary and middle school with minimal teasing, but problems could arise in high school, especially if he plays sports.

"And in the position of linebacker," the announcer shouts, "is Baaaby Evan!"

It will definitely be more difficult to intimidate his opponents if his "baby" name continues into his teenage years. But that's not all. My husband and I are concerned about his future career prospects as well. Will his name impede his professional goals if he decides to be a doctor, judge, police officer, or NASCAR driver? I can imagine all the potential hazards.

"Paging Dr. Baby Evan to the ER. Dr. Baby Evan, you are needed in the ER."

"All rise for the Honorable Judge Baby Evan."

"Officer Baby Evan to dispatch. I'm on the scene of a 10-30. Requesting back-up."

"And here they come 'round turn three. Who is that driving the Ford? Oh, yeah, buddy! I believe that's Baby Evan!"

Maybe we are getting a little ahead of ourselves. But it is time to start working with him on saying his real name. The other night we sat down and practiced.

"Your name is Evan Face," my husband said. "Can you say Evan Face?"

"Evan Face," our child repeated.

"Very good!" we praised.

Evan returned to pushing his tractors and shooting basketball. Then we called him back over to test our little lesson.

"What is your name?" my husband asked.

Evan paused thoughtfully for a minute.

"I'm Baby Face. I mean, I'm just Baby Evan."

"Evan Face," Craig reminded him.

"Yeah!" Evan said. And he returned to his toys.

I talked to my mom about the situation and she reminded me that almost everyone in my small hometown is known by a nickname.

"Imagine moving here, writing out Christmas cards, and trying to find names like Chicken Brown and Son Bailey in the phone book. Nobody is called by a given name in this town!"

I hadn't thought about that. Our town has a "Blinkee" and

a "Slic." Heck, even my dad has been known as "Moose" for the majority of his life. So, I guess Baby Evan will fit right in, as long as he lives in or around Wakefield. But, just in case he decides to move away from home, we will continue to practice, and hopefully he will learn his legal name.

And when he does, I will be so proud of my "baby," no matter how old he is.

WHEN SKIES ARE GRAY

I CROUCH at the bottom of the stairs and listen as Craig sings Evan to sleep.

"You are my sunshine, my only sunshine..."

It's a bit pitchy in places; my husband isn't a singer.

"You make me happy, when skies are gray..."

I strain to hear more, because I know the beauty in this song, and I know why he sings it. For our family, it is much more than a simple song.

My husband's mother died years ago. And though many memories have faded throughout time, Craig still remembers his mom lulling his brother to sleep with this tune. He might recall how her voice sounded, but he undoubtedly recollects how the song made him feel: warm and loved.

Last fall, Evan entered preschool and participated in his first musical performance for parents and grandparents. The program, entitled "You Are My Sunshine," began with the song by the same name. Along with his classmates, Evan stood straight and proud and confidently sang the familiar lyrics in a way that I had never heard before. It was hard to not cry.

While my precious preschooler sang out the words he had practiced for weeks, I thought back to my pregnancy and his birth. Evan was born just a few months after my father-in-law, David, passed away. David was able to pat my pregnant belly that summer. That was his and Evan's only earthly connection. His illness progressed rapidly, and David died in August. Evan was born the following November.

To say that his passing devastated the family would be a gross understatement. It was a trying, difficult time. How unfair it was for David to never meet Evan. How unfair for Evan to miss out on the love of a special grandparent.

We soon realized that Evan's birth brought light to a very dark time. The coos, smiles, and snuggles of a newborn warmed our souls. Evan made us happy when our skies were gray.

It's funny how we become attached to certain songs throughout our lives. And sometimes, we are so connected that it is difficult to separate life and music, conversations and lyrics. That is why the sound of a simple melody can bring on a smile or a torrent of tears. We are intertwined: the music is in us, and we are in the music.

Just a few months ago, I went online to create some wall art. I had a candid of Evan from a fall festival, and I wanted to turn it into a canvas. The photo is a close-up of his face, looking over his shoulder and smiling at me.

I perused the online merchandise for a template with an interesting quote or background. On the last page of options, I found it: a twelve by twelve canvas with the lyrics, "You Are My Sunshine" in the bottom left corner. I created the project and added it to my online shopping cart without checking the price. Sometimes cost is irrelevant.

Every now and then, these little pieces of sunshine surface in our lives. Sometimes they are on picture frames or Christmas ornaments, and we buy them when we can. Perhaps they are mere coincidences, perhaps a little something more.

I have lived long enough to experience my share of grief. I have known great loss. And because I have fought my way through darkness, it is easy to recognize the sunshine when it peeks through the clouds. I can feel it in a song. I can feel it in a memory. I can see it on Evan's face when he hands me a yellow flower on a rainy day.

ENOUGH STUFF

MY FRIEND, DAWN, put her house on the market last month. In order to prepare it for showings, she had to make a few repairs, do a bit of painting, and most importantly, get rid of some stuff.

Dawn cleaned out her son's room, putting a few things in storage and tossing some stuff in the garbage. When she was finished, her preschooler looked at his room and exclaimed, "Mommy! This is the best room ever!"

Instead of being sad that some of his toys were gone, he was thrilled to have more space to play.

I wasn't surprised to hear he was ecstatic. I know how I feel when I clean out a closet, organize a drawer, or purge an entire room. It's cathartic. It's incredible. It's like losing twenty pounds without having to diet. Why would we think children would feel any differently? Too much stuff clutters our homes, it overwhelms our minds, and it certainly interferes with a child's play.

In recent years, my husband and I have become very aware of the negative effects of too much stuff, and we have been fighting the impulse to buy. It's not an easy battle; messages to accumulate more pervade our lives. There are ads on TV, catalogs in the mail, and worst of all...adults! We are the ones who ask children what they want for their birthday. We encourage them to write a detailed list for Santa. We take them to toy stores and gift shops, then act appalled when they throw their little bodies in the middle of the aisle because we tell them they can't get anything.

I don't intend to live my life acquiring stuff—not for my children or for me. And in order to fight the stuff battle, I have had to be creative.

It was easy when my son was a toddler. Evan and I would spend an hour or so perusing the trains on the toy aisle. When he asked for one, I told him, "If we buy it, you won't have anything to look at the next time you come here." He was fine with that rationale. For the next few trips, he was content just looking.

As he has grown older, he has become more aware of what daycare buddies and school friends own, so I have to be more inventive.

Earlier this summer, Evan and I met my friend Sherry and her son Thomas at the movies. Afterwards, we walked to our cars and Thomas climbed in his mom's new vehicle.

"Want to see our new DVD player?" Thomas asked.

"Sure!" said Evan. "What are you watching?"

"*Tom and Jerry*. Do you have a DVD player in your car?"

"No," Evan said with regret.

I'm not opposed to DVD players. We just don't have one in our current vehicle, and buying one is not in the plans. That afternoon, Evan and I had a lengthy conversation about why we don't have some things and other people do.

Finally, I thought to remind Evan how much he enjoys pretending.

"We may not really have a DVD player, but you can pretend we do," I told him.

"You're right, Mom! Will you turn on the DVD player?"

I pressed the button for the interior lights, and Evan quickly thanked me.

"It's *Rescue Bots!*" he yelled. "Thank you for putting it on my favorite show!"

I realize that not all children enjoy pretend play the way my son does. There will come a time when my creative responses will turn into something more practical. I am prepared to eventually tell him that we don't have some things because we can't afford them or because we simply do not need them.

Please don't think that I deny my children their every request. I don't. We are not moving to Walden Pond anytime soon. I'm not even a true minimalist. I own more than one pair of jeans and more than one purse. And my kids have toys—plenty of toys. I just refuse to let stuff be the focal point of their lives. I don't want their happiness to be dependent on material items. I want them to collect experiences, not things.

We took our first beach trip as a family of four this summer. We stayed in an older, modest, oceanfront cottage on Topsail Island. I informed Evan before we left that this was not a souvenir-buying trip. The kids spent the week playing in the sand and collecting shells. When they weren't on the beach, they created with Play-Doh and blocks. It was perfect and completely relaxing.

One day, we needed to take a break from the sun, so we spent a few hours at an aquarium. The children enjoyed the jellyfish and seahorses. As we were leaving, we walked past the gift shop.

"Please, Mom?" Evan begged. "Can we go in?"

"We can go in, but we aren't buying anything," I reminded him.

"I don't want anything," he told me. "I just want to look."

That is exactly what he did. Evan looked at books, plastic sea creatures, stuffed turtles, and aquatic drinking glasses. He admired it all, and we left.

On the way home, we talked about our favorite things we saw. Evan was really excited about the sharks, but wished there had been some larger ones. I enjoyed the starfish; my husband liked the stingrays. The baby just said, "Fish. More fish."

We left without buying a thing—nothing to clutter the house, nothing that will end up in an eventual yard sale. Other than a bag of shells, we brought back nothing tangible. We just carried home an abundance of memories, something we always have room for.

WHY WE RUN

W‍HEN C‍RAIG and I signed up for a 5k race last winter, the first question our kids asked us was if we were going to win. Our older child, Evan, was especially concerned about how we would fare in the race.

"Well, do you think you will come in second?" Evan asked. "Or third?"

We explained to him that there were hundreds of people in the race and that many of them had been running a lot longer than we had. We told him that we just wanted to do our best and finish, and that it didn't matter what place we came in because that was not why we run.

"Why do you do it, then, if you don't want to win?" Evan continued.

My husband and I talked with him about the health benefits of running (for us, it's more of a jog) and the fact that it's something we both enjoy doing together. We also explained that there is a great sense of accomplishment in preparing for and completing a race. We told him that we like saving our race bibs, collecting medals, tracking our finish times, and trying to do better each time we run.

"I want to do one!" Evan exclaimed. "I already run some at school in gym, so I'm ready!"

We knew Evan wasn't ready for a three-mile race, but we

thought he could handle something shorter. So, when my alma mater hosted a 5k and kids' fun run, we asked Evan if he was still interested.

"Yes! Sign me up," he said. "I want to be an athlete."

We registered, paid our fees, and when race morning arrived, the three of us got ready together. Evan's fun run was first, and after some stretching exercises with the other children, the kids were on their way.

We watched as the children took off down the road and saw that Evan was trailing behind. At first, my heart sank just a little.

"What if he comes in last place?" I wondered. "Will he ever want to do it again?"

I hoped that my conversation with him about why I run had stuck with him and that he wouldn't care how he compared to the others. I hoped that he would just be happy with his own accomplishment, like his dad and I are with ours, but I know that a child's perspective is very different from an adult's.

We couldn't see Evan for a large portion of the race, but we were waiting, cameras ready, for him to cross the finish line. The first thing we noticed was a look of true determination on his face. His cheeks were red; his arms were pumping, and even though his legs were short, his spirit was enormous.

Evan beamed when he was given his medal at the end of his race, and he immediately placed it around his neck. Then he and his grandfather watched and cheered as Craig and I ran our 5k.

After our races, we ate snacks and watched the awards ceremony. None of us received an official award, but we all felt like champions. Evan had successfully completed his first race, and Craig and I had achieved personal records. What made it even better was we had shared the experience with our child.

Later that night, I peeked in Evan's room to see if he had gone to bed. He was standing by his dresser, taking pictures of his medal. I couldn't make out everything he was saying, but I did hear, "I guess this means I'm a real athlete now."

We were pleased with the way Evan reacted to his first race experience. He never mentioned that he was one of the last kids to finish (in his defense, he was also one of the youngest), and we didn't bring it up either. He is focused on his new athlete status, and he is anxious to run another race.

We are registered for our next event later this summer. This time, we are including our three-year-old, Delaney. Like a typical little sister, she saw Evan's medal and wanted one of her own. We told her the only way to get one is to run a race. She seems excited about running, aside from the fact that she has to wear socks.

We'll see how it goes. She may be able to walk the whole thing, or my husband might have to carry her across the finish line. Either way, we've found something that we like to do as a family. Races are fun, spirited events that often include music, free goodies, and food. Running and jogging are good for physical health and improving self-confidence, and you definitely don't have to win to feel great.

DREAM HOUSE

I TOLD one of my students that my husband and I were buying a new home.

"How exciting!" she commented. "Is it your dream house?"

"Not exactly," I answered, without thinking too much about it.

It isn't a dream house by HGTV's standards. It doesn't have an elevator, a guest house, or a media room. There is no dedicated shoe closet, backyard beach, or hydroponic garden.

Those features are extraordinary, but they are not "such stuff as my dream home is made on."

For the past few years, I have envisioned a large living space that didn't also hold our kitchen and dining areas. I have fantasized about how nice it would be to have a separate dining room and be able to host a real dinner party, complete with formal dishes and glasses. And more recently, I have dreamed about my children playing in a spacious yard that is not right next to a frequently traveled road.

My husband and I contacted our realtor this past February and began looking at a few properties online. We scheduled some visits and were just beginning to walk inside the second property when my realtor noticed my expression.

"It's only the second house you've seen," she warned. "Don't get excited too quickly."

"Oh, I'm not," I lied.

I faked minimal interest as we continued to tour the house. But in my mind, I had already moved in. My clothes were already hanging in the closet, and my book collection was displayed on the upstairs landing. My heart was invested in the house long before my money was.

The house was exactly what my husband and I were looking for. It had a private road and a wooded lot, elements we did not think possible when it was so close to the neighboring city. It had a large front yard, fenced back yard, separate dining area, and a fourth bedroom we could use for a playroom. It was perfect for our family of four.

Over the next few days, we made an offer, negotiated the price and closing costs a bit, then signed the contract. We waited for our loan to be approved, dealt with the home inspection and appraisal, and a few weeks later...it was our house.

In recent days, we have begun the arduous process of packing and moving our belongings. While cleaning out under my bed, I found a book of dream home plans that I bought from Lowe's several years ago. There was a time when we thought we might build our own dream home, and the book would serve as a source of inspiration. It has been under my bed ever since.

Flipping through the pages, I realized that my new home looked nothing like the plans in that book. Then I thought back to my student's question and realized I had answered her incorrectly.

The new house is our dream house. As we have grown older and had two children, our dreams have changed. Finding a home near a highly ranked school system has taken priority over spiral staircases and soaking tubs. A secluded road with minimal traffic ranks higher than skylights and window seats. The luxuries we once hoped to enjoy are no longer as important as having space to feed extended family and spend time with our children. What we are living in is better than a dream house: it's real. And it's ours.

DECK THE HALLS

I WANTED to buy a Christmas tree today. It was a department store tree, the already decorated variety. This silvery-white fir was adorned with matching bulbs and snowflakes, and it boasted a shimmering flake at the top. I thought about how much I would be willing to pay for such a tree, this quintessential symbol of the holiday season. Five hundred bucks? Seven hundred dollars? One thousand?

I fantasized about buying it, placing it (oh so gently) in the back of my SUV, and displaying it in my living room. I thought about not even removing the teeny, tiny barcode tags from all the lovely ornaments. They didn't bother me, and I didn't want to do any extra work. It was perfect just the way it was, aside from the fact that it wasn't for sale. And buying a ready-to-go, completely decorated tree would be a seasonal scam, a complete Christmas con. People are expected to trim their own trees.

Decorating is not fun for me. Each year, my husband brings the boxes of ornaments and other holiday decor from the attic and places them in our living room. I stare at them for a bit, then go fix a cup of cocoa. I return to the room and open a couple of boxes, look at a few ornaments, and watch a holiday film on Netflix. I clean the house, grade papers, and take a nap. I do anything I can think of to avoid decorating that tree.

Eventually, my husband becomes frustrated and starts placing the ornaments on branches. I watch from the sofa and tell him which ones are out of place. He moves them, and we have our first fight of the holiday season.

Just to be clear, I am not a scrooge. I love all things Christmas: music, parties, baked goods, and decorations. I prefer other people's decorations, though, because mine always look ridiculous. Always.

Take last year, for example. I was almost excited that we were going to try using garland for a change. I thought it might give our tree that tied-together look that it had been missing for nearly twelve years. We draped it loosely, then we tried it a bit tighter. I sank back on the couch, disheartened and defeated once again. Our living room looked like a hostage situation. Our tree wasn't trimmed; it was bound and gagged.

Somehow, we got past that moment, like we do every year. I like to think that something magical happens, but it may be that my incredibly patient husband works tirelessly with the lights and garland until it looks more like a Christmas tree and less like a crime scene.

Something was a bit different last year. Once our tree was finished, I began to admire its imperfections. I noticed its bent and broken branches, its disproportionate shape, and its burnt-out light bulbs. This time, I noticed with a less critical eye. This tree was so much like a human: imperfect by nature and judged by its beauty (or lack of).

This year, I am going to get past my decorating woes and fears of having an imperfect tree. My tree will not be perfect, and I'm going to embrace its defects. I also plan to take inventory of my life as I take out my ornaments.

A lot can change in a short time, and our situations are rarely the same from one Christmas to the next. We welcome new babies, say goodbye to loved ones, and sometimes part ways with friends. This year's tree will be a symbol of triumph. We made it through another year together, as a family. We made it through arguments, tears, sleepless nights, and celebrations.

We are here. We have the privilege of experiencing another holiday season together. What a great reason to deck the halls.

SOUL DEEP

"WELL, GOOD MORNING, CUTIE," the receptionist says to my daughter, Delaney, as we sign in for our appointment. She continues to compliment my daughter's looks, so I smile appreciatively and prompt Delaney to respond.

"Thank you," Delaney says on cue, and we find a seat in the waiting room, where she continues to receive compliments and kind remarks.

My daughter is beautiful. She has porcelain skin, a perfect pout, bright blue eyes, and blonde hair that curls at the ends. She epitomizes the ideal blonde beauty. She is only three years old, and I am a little worried for her.

I'm her mom, so naturally, I believe she is pretty. But this is more than a case of maternal prejudice. Store employees and businessmen frequently stop to chat with her.

"You've got a future Miss America on your hands there," one man told my husband.

Ladies stop us at the grocery store and the mall to tell her how attractive she is.

"Aren't you just beautiful?" one lady exclaimed. "Come here," she said. "I have something for you in my purse."

Then the lady gave Delaney five dollars and told her to buy herself something nice.

Delaney has an incredible personality in addition to her

good looks. She is very verbal, musical, and sarcastic. She is witty, clever, and quick to catch on to new concepts. But she gets noticed and receives attention because she is pretty. She is offered money, treats, and compliments based upon her physical appearance.

I can't help but wonder how she is processing this attention. What will she do with it as she grows older? Will she equate beauty to self-worth?

Because I teach teenagers, I have a little window into a world that could be my daughter's future. Some of my students have cosmetic bags larger than my suitcase. They perfectly apply liquid eyeliner, mascara, and false lashes. They paint their faces and nails, dye their hair, and tan their flesh. And they are only sixteen and seventeen years old. But somebody, at some point in time, sent the message that these products would make them more beautiful. So that is what they do.

A few years ago, I returned to my classroom from lunch and found one of my students crying at her desk. The boy she was dating had dumped her.

"He doesn't like that I cut my hair short," she sobbed into her notebook. "He doesn't think I'm pretty anymore."

I listened and told her that was not the case, and even if it were, it didn't matter what he thought. It was such a futile attempt at repairing her damaged self-esteem, and I knew it even as I uttered the words.

It does matter what people think and say about our appearance. It hurts when people make negative comments about our clothing, new hairstyle, or our weight. It stings when someone hints that we must be "expecting" because we have gained a little around the middle. Those comments are hurtful to an adult, so certainly they can be injurious to a teenager.

In the past year, I have lost a lot of weight. It was a change I wanted to make for myself in order to feel more comfortable and fully enjoy my life. I have received a lot of compliments since I began this journey, most of them from people who would love me no matter my size. Those are the ones that matter most. But one individual told me that I looked "Great—really skinny," and a part of me wondered if those two words meant the same thing.

I know that I am so much more than how I look. I know that real beauty comes from a place deep inside of me, and that weight loss, hair color, and makeup matter very little. That's what I want my daughter to understand. I want her to see herself as beautiful, regardless of what others see or say. I want her to accept compliments graciously, but realize deep down in her soul that only what she thinks is of real significance.

Delaney has decided to wear a hot pink tutu over her corduroy pants.

"How does this look, Mom?" she asks. She stretches her hands toward the sky and twirls across her bedroom floor. "Am I beautiful?"

Instead of responding the way I always have, I ask her how she feels.

"I feel great!" she says.

I admire her toddler confidence and wish I could bottle it up and store it for a time when she needs it most.

"You are great," I remind her. "And I'm glad you feel that way."

And, as her mom, I hope she always will.

WE LOVE YOU, MISS HANNIGAN

I RECENTLY WOKE UP from a dream in which I was starring as Miss Hannigan in a local production of the musical *Annie*. I messaged Dawn that morning and told her jokingly that it must be a subconscious hint for a new venture, and that maybe I should give acting a try.

A few minutes later, Dawn responded, "I just got in my car to go to lunch, turned on my radio, and Jay Z's 'Hard Knock Life,' was playing. No lie."

"It's totally a sign!" I wrote back.

"Right? What else could it mean!?"

I don't have a background in musical theatre. I'm neither an actress nor a singer, unless you count the kitchen productions I've starred in to entertain my children while they eat breakfast. But if those do count, I've played Dorothy from *The Wizard of Oz*, Roxie from *Chicago*, Sandy from *Grease*, and of course, all of the characters from my favorite musical of all time, *Annie*.

Even though my current audience is comprised of only two members, I don't hold back. I give them a full show, complete with choreography, props, and all the enthusiasm and stage presence a tired mom can muster. And they're worth it. They applaud and cheer; I've even had a few standing ovations.

My son, Evan, is most complimentary: "Mom, you are a really great performer," he says. "You need to be in a for real show."

This kid is the sweetest. And I like to think that he has great taste, but he also tells me I look beautiful in my bathrobe. Still, with so many critics in the world, every aspiring actress can use someone like Evan to keep her spirits soaring.

My obsession with *Annie* is one that stems from childhood. I can recall watching the movie for the first time in complete awe. I was terrified of Punjab, Daddy Warbucks, and Miss Hannigan. Annie, on the other hand, quickly became my idol.

I dressed as Annie for Halloween one year, complete with a blue cardigan, heart locket, and a horrible orange wig that I'd received as a birthday gift. I still have the locket; the wig had to go. I also had an *Annie* purse, nightgown, lunch box, and a few other accessories. I was the ultimate fan girl.

While it would have been amazing to have played Annie in my younger years, that dream is one that I can no longer entertain. But what about Miss Hannigan? That is still a possibility.

I can see myself lounging around the house in a silk robe and costume jewelry. Relaxing in the bathtub? You betcha. Shouting orders at children? I already do that every day! I am the ideal Miss Hannigan!

I do love the idea of starring in a production, but the reality of it is terrifying. I haven't been onstage since I was a junior in high school. And I've certainly never sung onstage. I would probably forget my lines, sing off-key, and eventually pass out from sheer embarrassment.

I'm much more comfortable performing in my own home, with my own small, yet appreciative, audience. I crave the applause of tiny hands and the cheers of little voices who simply adore their mother's version of "Little Girls" and how

I alter the lyrics to fit the most recent annoying thing they have done.

My kids love my singing and silly accents…for now. The day they stop clapping for me will be the day I seriously entertain the idea of a larger venue and a new audience. I may have no choice but to audition for the role of my favorite female villain. But first, I have to make these kids clean my floors…until they shine "like the top of the Chrysler Building!"

WHO PRESSED THE BUTTON?

I IGNORED my ringing phone, a number I didn't recognize anyway, and hopped in the shower. A few minutes later, Craig popped his head in the bathroom door.

"You missed all the fun," he said. "Our security alarm has been going off. It wouldn't take my code, and the police just left a few minutes ago."

"That explains the unfamiliar phone number on my caller ID," I told him. "It must have been the alarm company, and I ignored it."

Craig went on to explain that the alarm started screaming, and it wouldn't accept our four-digit code after several attempts. And because I didn't answer my phone, the police were automatically dispatched.

Three Prince George County officers showed up at our house, questioned my husband, and asked for proof of identification. Once they were confident that we were indeed the homeowners, they came into the foyer and chatted for a while with my husband and our two children. After a few minutes, they wished us a nice evening and headed on their way.

Craig and I were glad that they had left on a positive note. They didn't seem annoyed with us at all. Still, we were stumped about what had happened. We wondered what triggered the alarm, and we considered that perhaps it was malfunctioning. I decided I would call the alarm company the next morning.

When I was getting ready for bed that evening, I noticed a small, black object on my pillow. It was the remote to our security system. I keep it in the drawer of my nightstand in case of an emergency. Someone had obviously accessed it.

Craig and I called our children into the bedroom for questioning.

"I didn't do it," said six-year-old Evan. "I promise. I know that's only for emergencies."

"I not do it either," said three-year-old Delaney. Then, she took off down the hallway toward the playroom.

My husband and I exchanged a knowing look and went after Delaney. She denied pressing the button several more times before finally admitting she had done it.

"I'm sorry," she squeaked. But it was clear that she really didn't understand what she had done.

Craig and I agreed that we would try to find a way to help her understand that alarms are only for emergencies, and we cannot waste the time or resources of law enforcement.

About a week later, I decided that I would take Delaney to the police station so that she could apologize in person. But first we stopped at our local bakery and bought fresh doughnuts to take with us. I wanted to have her apologize for her actions and also thank the officers for responding to our home so quickly.

When we arrived at the station, the receptionist took our information and asked us to wait in the lobby. A few minutes later, four officers stepped out and introduced themselves.

Delaney was a bit overwhelmed by the sight of several officers in uniform, but she quickly got herself together, told them her name, and explained why we were there.

"I pressed the button," she said. "And I sorry."

The officers were very appreciative of her apology and the

treats we brought with us. They gave Delaney special coloring books and her very own badge to wear. She chatted happily with them and told them all about her brother and some recent boo-boos she had gotten.

Before we left, a staff member took pictures of Delaney with the officers, and later that day, the pics were uploaded to social media with a really nice caption about our visit. It turned out to be a positive experience.

I wanted Delaney to learn responsibility for her actions, but I also realize she is only three. It's hard to tell if it was truly a teachable moment or if she thinks that pressing the alarm button is a great idea—one that will result in another awesome field trip to the Prince George County Police Department.

BECOMING A REDSKINS FAN

I READ AN ARTICLE years ago about how important it is to appreciate gifts from children, especially those that are handmade. Children want to give, but they have neither the money nor the transportation to shop at a store. So, they make things for the people they care about. It is one of the purest expressions of love that exists.

My children are no exception. They draw, cut, color, and paste items from around the house, sometimes items that already belong to me. They present these items to us on holidays with so much pride, their faces literally glow.

Last July, my two kids handed me a gift bag on my birthday. I watched them nearly burst as I pulled out dozens of creations they'd made from napkins: hearts covered in stickers, cards with fringed edges, and cut-outs of our entire family. I told them that I loved everything they'd made and that I truly appreciated the thought and hard work that they put into their gifts.

Now that Evan is in elementary school, he has the opportunity to buy Christmas gifts through his school's Secret Santa Shop. Last December, we sent twenty dollars to school for him to shop for his sister, grandparents, father, and me. He came home that day, told us he had bought wonderful gifts, then went to his room to wrap them so they could go under the tree.

A few weeks before Christmas, Craig and Evan were watching a Steelers game. My husband has been a Steelers fan all his life. And though I really don't give a hoot about football, I echo his enthusiasm to keep things fun.

Throughout the game, Evan kept asking his dad questions about the Washington Redskins.

"Do you like the Redskins?" Evan asked him.

"No. Not really," my husband answered. "They have never been a team that I follow."

"Well, what would be your second favorite team?" Evan inquired.

"I guess if I had to pick a second favorite, I would say the Patriots, since I'm from New England."

"Oh. Okay. What is your third favorite team?"

"I'm not really sure, buddy. I've never thought about a third favorite team before. Maybe the Broncos."

"Okay," Evan responded.

Evan and his dad continued watching the Steelers game. Craig noticed that Evan had become quieter and appeared to be deep in thought.

Evan said, "I think my second favorite team is the Redskins."

"That's fine," Craig told him. "You can like any team you want."

"Washington is pretty close by, Dad," Evan rationalized. "We could easily go to one of their games."

"You're right, buddy. We sure could," Craig agreed.

A while later, the Steelers game wrapped up and Craig and Evan were throwing the football in the playroom. Evan blurted out, "Dad! I think I really messed up!"

"What's wrong, buddy? What do you mean?"

"All my school had for football gifts was Redskins stuff. So, I had to buy you a Redskins present for Christmas."

My husband's heart sank. He searched for words to console Evan. He told him that the Redskins were a great team and that they would make plans to go see them play one day.

Evan seemed satisfied, but Craig felt miserable. There is not much worse than seeing your child disappointed.

In the days leading up to Christmas, Craig and I made an effort to mention the Redskins in casual conversation. We talked about their record, how my great-grandfather was a faithful fan, and Evan and Craig looked online at player profiles. We did everything we could to make Evan feel better about his purchase.

On Christmas morning, the kids opened their gifts from Santa, enjoyed their stockings, and played with new toys. Then, Evan jumped up and yelled, "It's my turn to hand out gifts!" He went to the tree and grabbed his presents and passed them out.

The first gift he handed out was for his dad. Craig opened the square box and pulled out a Redskins bracelet.

"Do you like it?" Evan asked.

"I love it," Craig responded, as he slid it onto his wrist. "And it fits me perfectly."

The rest of Evan's gifts were also a hit, and our entire Christmas morning was one of the best we have ever had as a family.

Months have passed since Craig received his Redskins bracelet and became the team's newest fan. He still wears it every single day.

And when the day comes that it breaks and can no longer be worn, we will retire it to my desk drawer, where it will reside alongside our other treasures: handmade cards, napkin creations, and coloring sheets. It will be in good company, among the best gifts a parent could ever receive.

HOT DOGS FOR LUNCH

WE WERE in the mood for hot dogs and chips. I picked Delaney up from preschool, took her to the playground and the library, and asked her what she wanted for lunch.

"I would like a hot dog!" Delaney shouted. "And plain chips! Not the ones that are too hot in my mouth."

She was talking about the barbecue, and that was all they had on the counter of the local restaurant just down the road from her school. She asked me to buy them anyway.

Delaney and I sat across from one another and ate our hot dogs and chips. They were simple and delicious and exactly what my three-year-old wanted.

A lady sat down at a table next to ours and began eating her meal. "Those glasses sure are cute," she told my daughter.

"Thanks," Delaney said.

The lady asked if they were an accessory or if she had impaired vision, and I explained that Delaney is near-sighted and has astigmatism.

"Well, they look great on her," the lady emphasized.

I agreed.

"My baby has Asperger's," she told me. "He's in school now and doing really well because I got him started in programs early."

I commended her for being such a strong advocate for

her child and told her that I used to work with students with disabilities.

"He's actually my grandbaby," she said. "I thought I was done raising babies." She sighed and took a bite from her hot dog. "But what are you supposed to do when your daughter walks away from her own child?"

I just listened and took another bite of my hot dog.

"To her, it's like she just asked me to watch her purse while she went to the bathroom. No different, really."

She leaned her forehead against her palm and told me more about her family.

"My grandbaby's in kindergarten now, and he doesn't like the lunch, so I just feed him when he gets home, or I buy him a Lunchable. He knows what he wants and has a pretty strong sense of self."

We commiserated about picky eating habits and strong personalities. I knew exactly what she was dealing with in that respect.

"And my daughter has missed it all—the milestones, birthdays, Christmases. I don't know how it doesn't kill her soul. You know? It would kill your soul, wouldn't it?"

I told her it would, and I meant it. I know exactly how fortunate I am to be there for the major events in my children's lives. I am grateful to have every afternoon, evening, and weekend with them, and I really appreciate my special weekday lunch dates with Delaney.

Today, she chose hot dogs.

Delaney and I finished our lunch and moved on to dessert. At some point during our conversation, another customer had anonymously paid for Delaney's ice cream. We indulged and continued talking with our new friend.

"I lost a baby to SIDS years ago," she confided. "It's one of the most painful things you can imagine. I thought I had maxed out on my share of suffering; then my son committed suicide a few years ago. You may have heard of him. He was a decorated soldier from Prince George."

She pulled out a memorial poster from her purse. It was covered in pictures of him from high school and his time in the military. I told her that I never taught him, but some of my friends probably had. He was such a handsome and intelligent man, and he had achieved so much in such a short time.

I told her how sorry I was, and we chatted more about grief, pain, and loss. We both questioned how so many people go through life untouched by tragedy, yet others have to suffer endlessly. We talked about staying positive, working hard, and being grateful for the people we still have.

"My grandbaby is half white and half black," she continued. "He asked me where he fit in at school—if he fit with the black children or the white children. I told him he fit in with all of them because he's a human."

We both said we wished more people thought the way we do, and the world would be a better, safer place if they did.

When it was time to leave the restaurant, I wiped ice cream off Delaney's mouth and we all walked outside together. I told the lady how nice it was chatting with her and it was a lunch I wouldn't soon forget.

Delaney and I pulled out of our parking space and waved goodbye to our new friend, a lady I bonded with because of our beliefs on raising children and treating people with kindness. Our similarities far outweighed our differences, and I was so glad I had been there to listen to her story, the things she needed to say. It turned out I was the perfect person to hear it all.

Thank goodness Delaney chose hot dogs.

WHY I CAMP

"Why do you want to go camping?" Dawn asked.

I thought about the question.

I don't want to camp. I don't like it at all. My family didn't camp as a form of vacationing when I was a child; we stayed in hotels, like civilized people. Camping is really not something I long to do.

"I don't want to go camping," I told her. "But I also don't want to miss it."

Because my husband knows me well and realizes I can get a little grumpy in certain situations, he was wary when I asked to tag along on his family's annual trip to the Red Wing Roots Music Festival in Mount Solon, Virginia.

He feigned excitement as the date approached. I have to give him credit: he really appeared happy to have me there. But he and I both knew this trip wasn't about me. It was about our two kids and giving them the opportunity to spend time with their uncles and cousin. That is why I wanted to go.

When we arrived at the campsite, I had a beer (I like that part of camping) while my husband unpacked. Fortunately, his brother, Bryan, had set up our tent the day before, so Craig's workload was pretty light.

I looked around at the tents, gas lanterns, cooking equipment, and water filters, and I thought, *People spend a ton of money to live the way our ancestors did when they had no other choice.*

I kept my mood positive the first two days. I enjoyed the festival, the variety of food trucks, the beer garden, and family time. I loved staying up late by the campfire and getting as sleepy as possible in hopes that I would be somewhat unaware of the fact that I was sleeping on the ground.

It didn't work.

I remembered I was on the ground each time I turned over that night. And I turned over many times.

It rained on day three, all day and all night. It was still drizzling at bedtime, and though it was technically dry inside our tent, the dampness permeated the fabric. I felt it everywhere.

It is possible that I was a little grumpy that evening. I may have even suggested going to the nearest hotel. My lousy mood heightened later that night, when our car battery died. I wanted Craig to take us home right then, in case it died again, wouldn't recharge, and stranded us at the campground for the rest of our lives.

I imagined being stuck at the campsite forever, where I had to walk down a steep dirt path each time I needed to use the restroom and where I had to go to bed each night on the hard, damp ground.

Day three was miserable. It tested my patience and my ability to remain in a calm, pleasant mood. Others in our group weren't as bothered by the weather as I was. They are better campers than I am, or perhaps just better people.

So why did I go?

Why did I subject myself to a buggy bathroom, a damp tent, and no air conditioning in the middle of summer?

I did it because of the things I did not want to miss. My life has taught me not to miss the good things, if I can help it.

I didn't want to miss Evan holding a flashlight under his

chin, telling a spooky story by the campfire, while the rest of us tried not to giggle.

I didn't want to miss the excitement on Evan's face when his Uncle Scott took him to the front of the stage because The Steel Wheels were playing Evan's favorite song.

I didn't want to miss sassy Delaney, telling Uncle Scott he needed to "trim his beard," or watching her laugh until she got the hiccups because she had poured water on herself and everyone else during the first hour of the festival.

I didn't want to miss Evan eating grilled cheese sandwiches from the food truck three days in a row and saying it was the best thing he had ever tasted. I'm not a cook, so I wasn't the least bit offended by his comment.

I didn't want to miss witnessing the joy both of my children found in playing with Bryan's dog, putting twigs on the fire, and gathering rocks...just because.

I didn't want to miss the ice cream, kettle corn, pizza, s'mores, and doughnuts the size of small tires.

And I really didn't want to miss dancing with my daughter to "Angel from Montgomery," holding her close, twirling her around, and relishing in her littlehood.

The discomfort I endured was a small price to pay for what I would have missed if I had passed on this trip.

That is why I went camping. And why I will probably go again.

MOTHERHOOD

My daughter said her preschool teacher has a giant umbrella and she sticks the end in the ground so all the children in her class can play under it. That way they can still enjoy outdoor recess on rainy days.

My daughter said I need to practice my driving. "You don't even know how to get to California," she said. "But I know how."

"Is that right?" I asked. "How do you drive to California, Delaney?"

"It's easy. You go to Waverly, then Prince George, and there it is, just after Pop and Nanoo's house. California."

My daughter said, "That's the place, Mom! That's where the policeman got you. 'Cause you did the very, very bad U-turn. Did you almost go to jail?"

My daughter said she needed to draw something that begins with letter A for homework. She drew a fish, a bunny, and a cat.

"Those don't start with A, Delaney."

"'Animals does," she said.

My daughter said she was not on red at school today.

"It says on the app that you were," I argued.

"That's not true," she said.

"It says right here on ClassDojo that you were on red for

not using your words."

"No. That was someone else. That wasn't me."

My daughter said she couldn't be an angel in the Christmas Eve program.

"I'm not an angel," she insisted.

No joke, I thought.

"Can I be a cat?" she asked.

"There isn't a cat in the nativity scene," we told her.

"There should be," she said.

My daughter said she wrote something for me and I needed to hang it up by my desk at work. She handed me a square of yellow construction paper. She'd written "LOL CAT" in the center of the square. "Hang it up where your students will see it," she said.

My daughter said, "Thank you, Mommy," when I jumped into the pool and lifted her out of the water. It only took a second, just like they say. I had allowed her to take off her floaties, and she was holding onto a pool noodle. When a bug landed on her arm, she panicked, flipped off the noodle, and slipped beneath the surface.

For the next few minutes, we clung to each other and sobbed.

"Thank you," she said. "Thank you so much."

WEATHERING THE STORM

I KEEP HAVING the same nightmare: I'm outside in the middle of a severe storm, and I can't find Delaney. I call to her, eventually see her, but am unable to catch her. She reaches out to me, and each time I get closer, the wind takes her a little farther away and beyond my grasp.

I realize that these types of dreams are likely a manifestation of my anxiety, a problem I'm dealing with that is more challenging than I ever imagined and not at all unrelated to being Delaney's mother. But I also think this dream is a reminder of the incredible force of nature that my Delaney is: strong, unpredictable, and turbulent.

Returning to full-time work was a huge concern for me this year, because it meant that Delaney would need a full-time preschool situation. I feared her unruliness and defiance at home would carry over into the classroom. I worried about her saying inappropriate words and showing off her vast knowledge of potty humor. I worried about her refusing to wear her uniform. I worried about her back-talking her teacher. I worried about getting a call from the school during the first week saying, "Mrs. Face, it seems that our school is not a good fit for your daughter. We would rather our students not refer to each other as 'fart butts.' We wish you both the best in pursuing other educational opportunities. Please come get her."

I kept telling myself that if we could just survive this year, then she would be entering kindergarten and the law would REQUIRE that she attend school. Public schools would HAVE to take her, and I would be able to keep my job.

Delaney has been in school for almost nine weeks. So far, there has been no call.

She really hasn't had any negative reports, either, aside from one day of being on yellow for splashing water in the bathroom. She didn't defend her demerit, but instead said, "I'm disappointed in myself. I knew that it was bad, but I really wanted to splash." She has avoided being on yellow ever since.

The night before she began school, I read her *The Kissing Hand* by Audrey Penn. It's a story about a little raccoon who is nervous about being away from his mom when he attends school for the first time. Mama raccoon kisses her child's palm, then places it to his face. She explains that when he goes to school, he can touch his palm to his cheek and feel his mother's love.

After we finished reading the book, I kissed Delaney's palm and told her to hold it to her face if she missed me and needed to feel my love. "I will," she promised.

On the way to school a few days ago, Delaney told me to turn the music down. We were listening to "Wake Me Up Before You Go-Go" by Wham!. She wants to hear it every morning, and if we catch a few stoplights on Washington Street, we can play it a full three times from our house to her school. Yay!

"Turn it down, please," she repeated. "I need to tell you something."

"Okay," I said. "What's up?"

"You know how you gave me the kissing hand when I started school?"

"Yes. I remember."

"Well, I still have it. But I don't really need it right now."

"Why is that?"

"Because school is not new anymore."

It took me a few minutes to absorb her comment. She was telling me, in her way, that she had adjusted to her situation, and I didn't need to worry about her.

The neat thing about parenting, though, is that there is always something to worry about. We don't run out of opportunities to worry. We worry about our kids when they need us, and we worry about the day when they think they don't.

I'm happy and relieved with Delaney's adjustment to full-time school. My little force has new friends, a regular routine, and wonderful teachers. I think this is where my dream comes in, though. Delaney is establishing herself outside of her home and slowly slipping away from me. It is something to celebrate, and at the same time, something to lament. She will never be fully mine again. From now on, she will be influenced by her teachers and peers in addition to her father and me, and eventually, more so.

I can't help but worry about how hard this world is for females, and that I am raising a daughter in what is still, in many ways, a man's world. Then, Delaney talks, and I hear a little of myself come out. And I know. She will be able to stand up for herself and speak her mind. She's made of the tough stuff. She is my kid, and she's equipped to weather the storms. She will be okay. We both will.

I LOVE YOU MORE THAN COFFEE

"Do you like me more than candy?" Delaney asks. She's been on this kick for a few weeks now, partly joking and partly trying to determine how she measures up in our eyes.

"Of course I like you more than candy," I reassure her.

"Do you like me more than cookies?"

"Yes. I like you more than cookies, too," I promise.

"What about coffee?" Her expression turns serious. "Do you like me more than coffee?"

"Now that's a tough one!" I joke with her. "You wouldn't really ask me to choose between you and coffee, would you?"

Evan chimes in at that moment.

"Careful, Mom," he warns. "It's less than six days until Mother's Day. You don't want us to stop working on your presents, do you?"

I see him grin and wink at me in the rearview mirror, and I feel an actual ache in my chest from the love I feel for both of them.

"Of course I don't want you to stop. I adore the things you make for me."

But honestly, I had forgotten Mother's Day was approaching. As grateful as I am to have my children and to be their mom, I don't particularly love this holiday. Mother's Day makes me feel inept and guilty. It is a day of celebration of all the characteristics I don't demonstrate as a mom: selflessness, patience, tolerance, and kindness. It conjures images of moms who make and pack nutritious lunches, and plan and coordinate stimulating activities, all while talking in quiet, calm voices.

I tried to be that mom a few times. Twice, maybe.

Since I'm a relatively hopeful person, I have fleeting moments when I think I can still be that mom. I tried again last Friday.

Delaney asked me to make her pancakes for breakfast, so after dropping Evan off at school, we went to the McDonald's drive-thru, and I bought a large coffee and pancakes. That's how pancakes are "made" at this stage of my life.

We were both excited about our day together. I promised her I would color with her and play with her doll house. And I promised myself I would try not to yell or fuss the whole day.

Hilarious, right?

"Uh-oh!" Delaney exclaimed, while I poured her juice in the other part of the room.

Nothing good ever follows "Uh-oh."

"I spilled a little bit of syrup," Delaney whimpered.

"Of course you did," I said, not exactly to myself.

The entire packet of maple goo cascaded off the edge of the table, into Delaney's lap, and eventually formed an amber puddle on the floor.

For a minute or two, I just stood and watched it ooze and thought about what I might use to clean it up. I thought about not cleaning it up. I could just leave it there; we have other rooms in the house.

"I'm sorry," Delaney said. "I was just trying to be a big girl."

"I know," I told her, while I wiped syrup off her belly.

A few minutes later, my maple-scented daughter sat next to me with her box of crayons. We took turns coloring Skye from *PAW Patrol*, her current obsession, in as many shades of pink as we could find.

We were almost finished when Delaney told me she had to go to the bathroom. She has been working on her independence in this area as well, so she goes in alone, and I check on her as necessary.

After the sink had run for about five minutes, I knew it was time to check. I opened the door, and Delaney jumped.

"You scared me!" she said.

"It wouldn't be scary if you weren't doing something wrong," I scolded.

Delaney had her Doc McStuffins doll under the faucet, face upright. I wondered if she had been learning about water torture in preschool.

"What ARE you doing to your doll?" I demanded.

"I was just cleaning her face from where somebody marked on her."

That somebody was Delaney, about two weeks earlier.

I took in the scene: a puddle of water on the floor, two soggy towels on the door knob, and half a bottle of soap emptied into the sink, and Delaney, shirtless, perched on her stool, scrubbing away at Doc McStuffins' face. I'm still not sure why she took her shirt off for the task.

Anyway, my reaction was not one that I'm proud of, not one I aspired to back before I became a mother. Yelling, fussing, and tears erupted from both parties. I took Delaney upstairs to the bathtub, fussing all the way and wishing I could have just sat down and enjoyed my coffee, my coffee that sat cold on the counter, before the daily messes began, before I lost hope in another day, before I once again turned into the mom I do not want to be.

I was really hoping, as I scrubbed syrup, hand soap, and one unknown substance off my daughter, that she would not choose this moment to ask me if I liked her more than coffee.

This stage of life is so intense. Other working parents of

young children know what I mean. Stay-at-home moms and dads know what I mean, and my friends definitely know what I mean.

I received a text message from Dawn just the other day: "I've wiped poop off two different butts this morning and neither was my own," she said. "How is your day?!"

I laughed and commiserated. This is my life right now. It is nothing like I envisioned. I pictured myself having picnics, going to the park, and braiding my daughter's hair. But all of that seems like some fantastical scene from *Mary Poppins* and nothing like my actual life.

When I have been especially grumpy and critical of my children, I feel a nagging guilt, and I try to do something to make up for it. But last Friday, I just joked that maybe my kids could go to the Mommy Store and find a mommy who doesn't fuss so much.

Evan looked at me and said, "No way. I would never want another mommy."

My eyes met his, and I could tell that he meant it.

So, this year, I am going to try to be a little more enthusiastic about Mother's Day. I need to say farewell, forever, to the mother I thought I would be, and learn to appreciate the mother I actually am.

My children accept me in the same way I accept them, despite shortcomings. They know I have a temper. They know I can be impatient. They know I sometimes fail, yet they love me anyway. They call for me when they don't feel well and other times, too, like when they are mad at their father.

They are not perfect children, and I am not a perfect mom. But I love them something fierce, even more than coffee.

ACKNOWLEDGMENTS

THANK YOU, Evan and Delaney, for being constant sources of joy, love, laughter, and material.

Thank you, Delaney, for asking me if I loved you more than coffee and inadvertently giving me the title for this collection. I love that you had a really good idea of where you fit in my life.

Thank you, Craig, for your unwavering support. I am grateful for the quiet time and space that you provide me in a world that is rarely quiet and always short on time. I am so happy we are doing this life thing together.

Thank you, Wayne and Kim, for your unconditional love and patience. I know I was not an easy child to raise, and I am grateful we can laugh about those years now. Thank you for grounding me and encouraging me to use a pen more often than a telephone.

Thank you to the editors who published early excerpts of this collection:

"Sleepless Nights" Story by Melissa Face, *Chicken Soup for the Soul: Parenthood*. (c)2013 Chicken Soup for the Soul, LLC. All rights reserved.

"Sleepless Nights" Story by Melissa Face, *Chicken Soup for the Soul: For Mom with Love*. (c)2016 Chicken Soup for the Soul, LLC. All rights reserved.